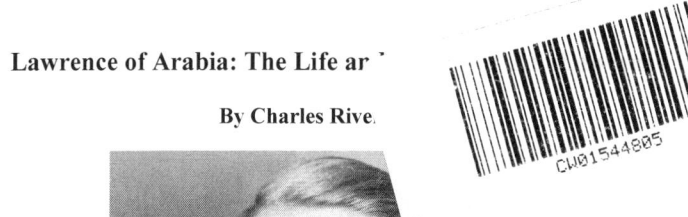

Lawrence of Arabia: The Life and Legacy

By Charles Rivers

About Charles River Editors

Charles River Editors provides superior editing and original writing services across the digital publishing industry, with the expertise to create digital content for publishers across a vast range of subject matter. In addition to providing original digital content for third party publishers, we also republish civilization's greatest literary works, bringing them to new generations of readers via ebooks.

Sign up here to receive updates about free books as we publish them, and visit Our Kindle Author Page to browse today's free promotions and our most recently published Kindle titles.

Introduction

T.E. Lawrence (1888-1935)

"I've been & am absurdly over-estimated. There are no supermen & I'm quite ordinary, & will say so whatever the artistic results. In that point I'm one of the few people who tell the truth about myself." – Lawrence of Arabia

He was recognized by many as a curious scholar and archaeologist, brilliant linguist, British soldier, extraordinary adventurer, and avid writer, though he called himself an "ordinary man." He was a gifted translator, a shrewd diplomat, a brilliant tactician, and an instinctive leader. T.E. Lawrence, more popularly known as Lawrence of Arabia, was a seminal figure in the shaping and reshaping of the politics of Arabia in the early 20th century, serving as an expert in Arab affairs in the British military and playing a key role in the Great Arab Revolt of 1916-1918.

World War I, also known as the Great War of 1914-1918, was one of the deadliest conflicts in human history, leading to the deaths of millions of soldiers and civilians, and it was a war that produced too many casualties and too few heroes. However, after the war was over, the world was told of the blonde-haired, blue-eyed British officer named Thomas Edward Lawrence, and his experiences in Arabia during the fighting. Pictures of Lawrence in a flowing white robe of Arabia's Bedouin tribes were distributed, and Lawrence's autobiography, *Seven Pillars of Wisdom*, further catapulted his fame and sensationalized his public image. Lawrence's story served to boost the spirits of many who were struggling to recover after the tragedy of the war.

It is telling of just how remarkable the tale is that the world's fascination with Lawrence of

Arabia has endured today. Articles, books, films, and documentaries about Lawrence and his exploits are continuously released on an annual basis. Historian Phillip Knightley once commented, "Along with Winston Churchill, [T.E. Lawrence] remains perhaps the best-known Englishman in the world." Decades since the end of the war, and with a completely changed Middle Eastern geopolitical landscape, Lawrence of Arabia and his legacy are still remembered and referenced as politically, militarily, and socially pertinent. As one of his biographers, Michael Korda, wrote in *Hero; The Life and Legend of Lawrence of Arabia*, "Today, when the Middle East is the main focus of our attention, and when insurgency, his [Lawrence's] specialty, is the main weapon of our adversaries, the story of Lawrence's life is more important than ever."

However, Lawrence was by no means everything he claimed to be. Like many great men touched by fame and celebrity, he exaggerated some details, underplayed others, and strove to maintain an image of himself that he had created in his own mind. Thus, Lawrence was and still is a very controversial figure. He was the first in the 900 year history of the British monarchy to refuse a knighthood, and the film *Lawrence of Arabia*, starting Peter O'Toole as Lawrence and widely lauded as a masterpiece, was banned in many Arab and Middle Eastern countries, including Jordan and Turkey. Turkey especially has long vilified Lawrence, questioning the veracity of many of his accounts. Just recently, in October 2014, Turkish President Recep Tayyip Erdogan went so far as to declare T.E. Lawrence a greater enemy than the radical terrorist organization that is operating in Iraq and Syria, the Islamic State (IS). In a furious anti-Western diatribe, Erdogan described Lawrence as an "English spy disguised as an Arab," and he warned of the threat posed by modern-day Lawrences in Turkey "disguised as journalists, religious men, writers, and terrorists" who are allegedly aiming to destabilize the country and region.

Another element of his polemical nature results from Lawrence's enigmatic personality. The young soldier was brilliant and brave, and boisterous and aggressive when he needed to be, but he was also quite private, reclusive, and hidden. Scholars and historians have squabbled over this true nature, asking whether he was courageous or reckless. Was he a true hero or a fortunate opportunist? Was he a true supporter of Arab independence, or a man seeking self-aggrandizement?

Lawrence of Arabia chronicles the life and legacy of one of the most famous heroes of World War I. Along with pictures of important people, places, and events, you will learn about T.E. Lawrence like never before, in no time at all.

Lawrence of Arabia: The Life and Legacy of T.E. Lawrence

About Charles River Editors

Introduction

   Chapter 1: Early Life of Thomas Edward Lawrence

   Chapter 2: Archaeology in the Middle East

   Chapter 3: The Start of Lawrence's Military Career

   Chapter 4: The Start of the Arab Revolt

   Chapter 5: The Capture of Aqaba

   Chapter 6: The End of the War

   Chapter 7: Lawrence's Fame and Later Years

   Chapter 8: The Death and Legacy of Lawrence

Bibliography

Chapter 1: Early Life of Thomas Edward Lawrence

The birthplace of T.E. Lawrence

"All men dream: but not equally. Those who dream by night in the dusty recesses of their minds wake in the day to find that it was vanity: but the dreamers of the day are dangerous men, for they may act their dreams with open eyes, to make it possible. This I did." – Lawrence of Arabia, *Seven Pillars of Wisdom*

Thomas Edward Lawrence was born on August 16, 1888 in Tremadoc, Caernarvonshire, Wales. He was the second son of Sir Thomas Chapman – the son of a prominent Anglo-Irish landowner and the last of the Chapman baronets – and Sarah Junner, who was Sir Thomas's daughters' governess. What was little known until after Lawrence's fame exploded post-WWI was the fact that Lawrence and his four brothers were illegitimate. Sir Chapman had already been married to a woman named Edith in Ireland when he fell in love with Sarah Junner, but when he requested a divorce, Edith pointedly refused to accept one. Thus, Sir Chapman fled Ireland to set up a new family and home with Sarah Junner, and the couple, who were unable to marry, renamed themselves "Mr. and Mrs. Lawrence." The world in the 1800s was vastly different from our world today; there was hardly any need for official documents to prove one's identification, and the process itself was not systematized. It was therefore fairly easy for the couple to adopt a new identity simply by calling themselves by a different surname. In 1896, the Lawrence family settled in Oxford, where Lawrence attended school and college.

The couple's secret about their illegitimate relationship was a serious one in those times. Thomas Lawrence's real name was Thomas Robert Tighe Chapman; he had been a prominent member of the Anglo-Irish landed aristocracy, and he already had four daughters with his wife, Edith. His relationship with Sarah Junner grew out of an affair; by the time Edith discovered the truth, Sarah had already given birth to their first son, and she was already pregnant with the second. That Sir Thomas chose his mistress over his wife and not only fled from his family, but also gave up all claims to his family inheritance, was especially scandalous in those times.[1]

The Lawrences' decision to move to Oxford was thus a difficult and harrowing one. In the countryside of Wales, the family could maintain some degree of anonymity, but in a bustling city like Oxford, the couple were bound to run into someone from their past or someone who knew about the scandal, as the story of Thomas running off with his daughters' governess had reached the ears of many people among those of his class in London. And yet, Thomas, as a well-educated man with an aristocratic background, knew the value of a good education. The couple decided to take the risk and relocate to the university town of Oxford so that their five sons can receive a good education.

Exactly when and where Lawrence and his brothers each found out about this family secret is unclear. However, it undoubtedly impacted Lawrence, as his biographer Michael Korda noted: "There is no doubt that this background played a major role in forming Lawrence's character and shaping his desire to become a hero. A powerful combination of shame, guilt, and ambition drove him to seek a fame brilliant enough to make the name Lawrence more worthy than the name Chapman, and thus to offer his father, the aristocrat who had put aside his title and wealth to run away with his daughters' governess, a hero for a son."[2]

At the Oxford High School for Boys, young Lawrence stood out as an exceptionally bright student, but his bashfulness and reclusive nature were also noted. "Ned," as he was called by his friends and family, also stood out because of his adventurous nature; much of this can likely be attributed to the strictness with which his mother ruled the house. Sarah Lawrence, described as a "domestic tyrant," was an energetic and vivacious woman, but also a relentless disciplinarian, to such a degree that Lawrence must have felt suffocated. Sarah was especially hard on Lawrence, as he was more self-challenging and curious than his brothers, which often appeared in the forms of naughtiness and disobedience. Sarah may have also focused on Lawrence the most because of his apparent lack of religiosity. Sarah Lawrence, though not as religiously fervent as Edith Chapman had been, still placed great emphasis on her faith; that she had broken up a marriage and birthed five illegitimate sons no doubt played a large role in her efforts to impose on herself and on her sons strong religious feelings. Though she succeeded with four of her sons, Ned did not have an inkling of a religious spirit, which made her work all the more harder to "save" him.[3]

---

[1] Scott Anderson, *Lawrence in Arabia: War, Deceit, Imperial Folly and the Making of the Modern Middle East* (New York: Anchor Books, 2014), 4.
[2] Korda, *Hero,* 114-115.
[3] Ibid., 124-127.

A memorial plaque to Lawrence at Oxford High School for Boys

While his brothers continued to grow tall as they passed through adolescence, Lawrence stopped growing at around the age of 15. Many think of Lawrence to be a lean and towering figure, likely because he was played by the six-foot-tall Peter O'Toole in the widely distributed film *Lawrence of Arabia*, but in reality, Lawrence was only 5'3-5'5. Given that his brothers, even his younger ones, were all taller than him, this undoubtedly increased his already pronounced shyness.[4] This reticence displayed itself in Lawrence's absolute disdain for any kind of team sports. At school, he did everything he could to avoid any and every form of organized competition.

At the same time, it would also be erroneous to categorize Lawrence's early years as isolated and reclusive, or think that young Ned was a misfit at Oxford High School. Though Ned Lawrence was a loner and preferred solitary studies to following an established curriculum or playing team sports, he had many friends with whom he had healthy relationships. Additionally,

---

[4] Anderson, *Lawrence in Arabia*, 21.

it became evident to the teachers there that Ned Lawrence was something of a genius, a prodigy even, which was difficult to ascertain at first because he was so unfocused on his studies. Like many bright children, Lawrence found it difficult to concentrate on subjects and topics he did not find interesting, and instead pored over material that sparked his interest, despite the fact that many of these were outside the curriculum.

One of these interests was archaeology. In Oxford, Lawrence often spent his free time walking around the city admiring the buildings, churches, and museums. At the age of 15, Ned, with a friend, bicycled around Berkshire and Oxfordshire and visited almost every village's church, studied their monuments and antiquities, and made rubbings of their monumental brasses.[5] He frequented the Ashmolean Museum so often that he grew close to the curators there, and he presented his archeological findings and rubbings to the museum, earning him a curious reputation there. In 1906, he took an extended bicycle tour of the castles and cathedrals of Normandy, and in 1907, when he was admitted to Jesus College of Oxford University to study history, Lawrence wrote his thesis on the architecture of medieval castles and fortifications, an early indication of his interest in military history. For this thesis, he conducted research by taking another bicycle trip across France to visit more castles, which opened his eyes further to the greater world around him.

In the summer of 1909, Lawrence embarked on a three-month walking tour on which he trekked 1,000 miles on foot. He travelled across Syria, Palestine, and parts of Turkey to visit 36 crusader castles, according to his accounts. The notes he made on this trip contributed to his thesis, which was entitled "The Influence of the Crusaders on European Military Architecture – to the End of the XIIth Century." In 1910, Lawrence graduated with a first class degree in history and was awarded a research fellowship by Magdalen College.[6]

One of the most important figures Lawrence met in Oxford who would later greatly impact his life was David Hogarth, a renowned scholar, writer, and archeologist. In 1908, Hogarth became keeper of the Ashmolean Museum, where Lawrence had frequented since his early teenage years. It was here that Hogarth met Lawrence, who was helping the assistant museum keeper arrange the medieval pottery, and took an interest in him. This was the beginning of a fruitful relationship for Lawrence; Hogarth was well travelled and well connected, and an excellent scholar of the Middle East. Though three times Lawrence's age, Hogarth passed down to Lawrence all his experiences, knowledge, and ideas, inspiring young Lawrence and stimulating him to actively pursue his own interests. Lawrence would later describe Hogarth as "a very kind, very wise, very loveable man…I'd put him high among the really estimable human beings. All my opportunities, all those I've wasted, came directly or indirectly, out of his trust in me."[7]

---

[5] C.F.C. Beeson and A.V. Simcock, *Clockmaking in Oxfordshire 1400--1850 (3rd ed.)* (Oxford: Museum of the History of Science, 1989), 3.
[6] Petri Liukkonen, "Who's Who – T.E. Lawrence," *FirstWorldWar.com*, accessed November 1, 2014, http://www.firstworldwar.com/bio/lawrencete.htm.
[7] John E. Mack, *A Prince of Our Disorder: The Life of T.E. Lawrence* (Boston: Harvard University Press, 1998), 58-

It was natural then that he would join Hogarth's archaeological expedition as a junior assistant in the ruins of Carchemish, an ancient Hittite city located along the frontier between Turkey and Syria. The excavation was being set up by Hogarth on behalf of the British Museum, and it was an important one; though the fact that an entire ancient city can be unearthed was certainly a compelling reason for the British interest, these were also the pre-war years, when rivaling countries took their political competition into other fields, including the arts. The Germans and the University of Berlin had made great archaeological discoveries in Anatolia in 1906-1907, which spurred the British to pursue discoveries of their own in the region.[8] Hence, the Carchemish dig had not only archaeological motives, but political ones as well.

Lawrence (left) and Hogarth (center)

It was for this archaeological pursuit that Lawrence would spend an extended period of time not only in Carchemish, but also across Syria, Egypt, and Palestine. This period away from the environment he was born and raised in was important for him, as this was when he made connections with those who would influence him greatly the rest of his life. Additionally, it was also when his affinity for the Middle East was developed and strengthened, transforming his

---

[8] Korda, *Hero*, 173.

interests from purely academic and scholarly to political and personal.

Chapter 2: Archaeology in the Middle East

"Feisal asked me if I would wear Arab clothes like his own while in the camp. I should find it better for my own part, since it was a comfortable dress in which to live Arab-fashion as we must do. Besides, the tribesmen would then understand how to take me." – Lawrence of Arabia

For centuries, much of Arabia had been under the rule of the Ottoman Empire. The Ottoman army in the region, called the Army of Arabia (Arabistan Ordusu), was based at Damascus and oversaw Syria, Cilicia[9], Iraq, and the Arabian Peninsula.[10] Thus, at the outbreak of WWI, most of Arabia was part of the Ottoman Empire, with the exceptions of the British protectorates of Kuwait, Aden, Hadramawt, and the Omani coastlines. Simply put, the Middle East as it is known now did not exist in the early 1900s.

Since the Ottoman Empire covered such a vast swath of territory, its population was composed of citizens of varying ethnicities, languages, cultures, and religions. The ruling family was Turkish, but citizens of the Empire included Turks, Arabs, Kurds, Greeks, Persians, with religious groups like Sunnis, Shi'ites, Christians, and Jews. The Ottoman Empire ruled with an iron fist to maintain control over such a diverse population, which translated into draconian laws, forced conscription into the Ottoman army, and the subsequent emergence of Arab nationalism.

The years preceding the outbreak of WWI saw a great increase in discontent among the population of the Ottoman Empire. This was spurred further by radical changes in the Ottoman government itself, as the Young Turk Revolution that began in July 1908 transformed the political field and led to increased instability. Sultan Abdulhamid II was dethroned, and power shifted into the hands of the Young Turks' Committee of Union and Progress (CUP). The new secular government placed even greater political and social restrictions on its people in an attempt to "Turkify" the empire, instigating further discontent, as many began to realize that the Ottoman Islamic Empire had been replaced by a Turkish Empire.[11] Military setbacks followed, further destabilizing the new government. In 1908, Turkey lost Bosnia-Herzegovina to Austria-Hungary, and a failed campaign in North Africa in 1911-1912 led to its losing Libya to Italy. To make matters worse, in 1912, after the First Balkan War, Turkey lost Macedonia. The empire was slowly heading toward collapse.[12]

In a number of cities, such as Mesopotamia and Damascus – traditional cities of learning and scholarship – secret societies opposing the government were formed, with some contemplating revolt. Crackdowns on these societies followed in 1914-1916, which led to the execution of

---

[9] Also known as Kilikia, this area corresponds to the southeastern coast of modern Turkey. It existed as a political entity from Hittite times into the Byzantine Empire.
[10] Stanford J. Shaw and Ezel Kural Shaw, *History of the Ottoman Empire and Modern Turkey* (Cambridge: Cambridge University Press, 1977), 85.
[11] David Murphy, *The Arab Revolt 1916-18: Lawrence Sets Arabia Ablaze* (Oxford: Osprey Publishing, 2008), 5-6.
[12] Ibid., 6.

several of their leaders. In addition to this, further south in the deserts of Arabia, tribes began organizing to demand reform, particularly of the new government's taxation policies.

However, it is important to note that while Arab nationalism was beginning to take hold among many – particularly the educated in the major cities of Damascus, Beirut, and Cairo – it was hardly a mainstream ideology or a mass movement. Many Arabs were still loyal first to their religion, ethnicity, or tribe. The ideologies of Ottomanism and pan-Islamism were therefore still dominant ideologies; it is safe to say that those advocating a revolt and complete separation from the Ottoman Empire were a small minority.

This was the political and social environment in which Lawrence came into contact with local workers, tribes, and scholars while at the Carchemish site. Without a more unified force, the Arabs hoping for change in the current circumstances would not be able to succeed in any attempts at revolt. Furthermore, another important point to take note of is that though the Middle East was important in that it was a game board in which political competition and rivalries were played out, it was only of marginal concern to the great nations in the early years of the 20th century when these rivalries were seemingly resolved. Oil had not been discovered in Arabia (though it was discovered in Persia in 1908), and thus, unlike the geopolitically and economically strategic Middle East of today, the Middle East of the 1800s and early 1900s was essentially a political backwater.[13]

Lawrence arrived in Beirut in December of 1910 and immediately traveled to Jebail, the ancient Greek city of Byblos, where he studied Arabic with a teacher named Fareedeh for nearly two months. He was able to reestablish some semblance of a stable life here, after a long trip to Beirut. Letters sent by him to his family and vice versa show how close he truly was with his family, despite many attempts to psychoanalyze Lawrence's supposed isolation from his family, and especially his mother. In these letters, he described his life in Jebail at length to his family, and his parents in turn would tell him everything about life back in Oxford – so much so that the "entire Lawrence family seems to have been engaged in writing an endless series of letters and postcards."[14]

Lawrence's short time with his Arabic instructor, Fareedeh, allowed him to brush up his Arabic, though he was apparently nowhere near fluent at this time. Later, Fareedeh would describe Lawrence after he achieved fame as having been "like an oyster which has, through pain and suffering, all through life developed into a pearl which the world is trying to evaluate, taking it to pieces layer by layer, without realizing the true value of the whole." Biographer Michael Korda responded to this with an astute observation: "There is some truth to this [Fareedeh's comment], even today. Lawrence's detractors and admirers alike tend to dissect his personality into thin slices, separating the soldier from the scholar, the hero from the teller of tall tales, the

---

[13] David Fromkin, *A Peace to End All Peace: The Fall of the Ottoman Empire and the Creation of the Modern Middle East* (New York: Henry Holt and Company, 1989), 25.
[14] Ibid., 176-177.

victim of neuroses from the man of action, and in the process losing sight of just what an attractive and interesting person he was, even at his most infuriating. Fareedeh clearly recognized this, and understood early on that Lawrence was always more than the sum of his parts. Provocative as Lawrence could be, there was about him a certain sweetness of disposition, a spiritual quality, and above all a sense that he was a special person, destined for greatness, even though it was not yet clear what kind it would be."[15]

When Lawrence arrived in Carchemish with Hogarth and others of the excavation team, he was fully in his element. As the team set up on site, Lawrence was in the midst of activity, laboring and digging, overseeing the work when Hogarth was away. He also worked on his Arabic and cultivated his love for writing; it was during his travels here that Lawrence began what was to become a lifelong habit of writing his thoughts, observations, and opinions, occasionally sending letters to the editors of newspapers in Britain. Some of these letters to the editor were especially critical; the very first letter that was published was printed in the *London Times*, and it was a severely biting attack on the Turkish government and its allowing foreign developers, particularly the Germans, to tear down precious archeological sites and antiquities.[16] This article was to become a precursor for Lawrence's lifelong condemnation of the Turks.

Lawrence began his trip home in August of 1911. He was ill and was still weak when he arrived home, but as soon as he recovered, he set out again to Carchemish against the wishes of his doctor. There, he met Charles Leonard Woolley, who had been assistant keeper of the Ashmolean Museum in Oxford. He and Woolley would become close friends and colleagues, and Woolley himself would continue to lead an illustrious career.

---

[15] Ibid., 175-176.
[16] Ibid., 186.

Pictures of Lawrence and Leonard Woolley circa 1912-1913

Lawrence and Woolley at the Carchemish site

By this point, Lawrence was quite fluent in Arabic, and beyond his linguistic interest, he had developed a deep affinity for the Middle East – its culture, its people, its language, and its customs. While those like Woolley were more focused on the excavation and discovery, Lawrence spent significant time with the local men, honing his Arabic and questioning, observing, and taking notes. His leadership skills grew immensely during the Carchemish expedition as well; Hogarth was away quite often, and with Hogarth not present, it was often up to Lawrence to manage the work teams and oversee the digs. The fact that Lawrence naturally became a leader of the dig was partly due to his status as a European, and the culture of European interference, influence, and imperialism in the Middle East. However, it was also because he fit in well with this seemingly foreign environment; from the information he gathered from the locals, Lawrence began charting out the complicated clan structure and tribal relations that determined regional politics in this remote area of Syria. Moreover, he gained the respect of locals as he "seemed to have none of the softness or frailty they associated with Europeans; rather, he could work in the blazing heat for hours without pause, could walk or ride for days without complaint, soldiered through bouts of dysentery and malaria with the composed resignation of a local."[17]

One other figure Lawrence met who would influence him and his life greatly was a young boy

---

[17] Anderson, *Lawrence in Arabia*, 33.

from Jerablus named Dahoum. Starting out as a "water boy," the young Dahoum was recognized by Lawrence for his sharp wit and curious nature, though he was illiterate. Lawrence took him on as something of his personal assistant, and even brought him home with him to Oxford in 1913. Dahoum has often been described as attractive, and as "beautifully built and remarkably handsome," particularly by Lawrence himself. It was Lawrence's closeness with the young boy that spurred questions back then about his sexual orientation, and this has continued to be the subject of much debate and speculation.[18] Regardless of what the true nature of the relationship between Lawrence and Dahoum was, Dahoum became an important part of Lawrence's fixation on, and his ties to, this region of the Middle East.

Eventually, the world changed into a different place as tensions between countries began mounting, sparking several conflicts across Europe. Rumors of the start of a global war reached even the remote piece of desert that Lawrence and his team were occupying. In January 1914, Lawrence and Woolley were presented with an offer for an adventure that Lawrence could scarcely give up, demonstrating his shift from purely academic pursuits to fulfilling his thirst for adventure.

The British Palestine Exploration Fund (PEF) was founded in 1865 as an organization tasked specifically for the study of the Levant, which was the southern area of what was conventionally known as Palestine.[19] Though the Fund had initially been set up to map areas of biblical importance, the strategic importance of the meticulous inch-by-inch maps that the Fund created was soon recognized by the British government. As tensions increased between Germany and other European countries, and as Germany intensified its diplomatic efforts to incorporate Turkey into the alliance that would soon become known as the Central powers, the urgency of having a detailed map of Palestine increased – especially for areas like the Sinai Peninsula, a key area that the Turkish army would undoubtedly hope to cross to seize the strategic Suez Canal. The Fund was therefore tasked with completing the survey of Palestine – particularly, the vast deserts of Zin, which had been completely overlooked and unmapped.

However, any such exploration of these lands would require permission from the Turks. In order to secure this, the Fund asked the British Museum, which was involved in the Carchemish dig, to send Lawrence and Woolley on a mission to map the little-known but militarily strategic area of Zin, Palestine, under the guise of an archaeological mission. Though for Lawrence and Woolley, this was more an archaeological pursuit than an intelligence mission, Lawrence especially was excited to uncover biblical routes leading from Egypt to Palestine.[20] The Fund made sure to stress the mission's archaeological nature and its biblical significance, so that Turkish authorities would not know the true nature of this mapping mission.

Lawrence, along with Woolley, was authorized to conduct their mission into Zin, so in the span

---

[18] Korda, *Hero,* 184.
[19] "About Us," *Palestine Exploration Fund,* accessed November 1, 2014, http://www.pef.org.uk/about/.
[20] Jennifer Speake, *Literature of Travel and Exploration: An Encyclopedia* (London: Routledge, 2003), 701.

of less than two months, the two men trekked across much of the Negev Desert and the Wadi Arabah, recording, mapping, and documenting as they went along. The results of their research of the wilderness of Zin were published in the annual report of the Fund in 1914-1915.[21] Lawrence's true motivations behind this mission are unclear. Whether his primary concern was a thirst for adventure, a want of knowledge, loyalty to his country, or a mixture of all of these, Lawrence was immensely satisfied with the fact that he had been chosen for such a clandestine mission.

On June 28, 1914, Austrian Archduke Franz Ferdinand was assassinated, a staggering event that triggered one of the greatest tragedies of the history of the world – World War I. Like almost every other family in Britain, and in the region, the war transformed Lawrence and his family. Frank, the second youngest in the Lawrence family, was taken into the Gloucestershire Regiment, as he had attended the Oxford University Officers Training Corps. Bob, the eldest son, joined the Royal Army Medical Corps, as he had been studying in medical school.[22] Like so many others, they did not expect this war to last for years, nor did they or anyone in Britain at the start of the war expect it to claim millions of lives, making it one of the greatest human tragedies in the history of the world.

Lawrence briefly considered volunteering to join the British army to participate in the war, but several factors held him back. The first was a practical reason; Lawrence stood well below the War Office's minimum height requirement. Secondly, young men were enthusiastically volunteering by the thousands; there was an excessive amount of young volunteers waiting to be trained, which was part of the reason the War Office had made the height requirement stricter, among other requirements. Thirdly, the British Palestine Exploration Fund was being urged to publish its findings as soon as possible. As enthralled with military offensives as Lawrence was, and as much as he preferred adventure to purely scholarly work, Lawrence decided to continue working with the Fund. Finally, despite having signed a secret alliance with Germany, the Turks had not yet declared war on the Allied powers, and there was vigorous negotiating between the two sides. The British were thus even more determined to keep the fact that the Fund's mapping project was a military expedition rather than an archaeological one a secret, so it was in the British government's interests that Lawrence and Woolley not join the army and continue as scholars and archaeologists. Lawrence went so far as to contact Stewart Newcombe, his supervisor on the Fund expedition and a ranking office in British military intelligence, to inquire about positions there. He was politely refused and told that if Turkey entered the war on Germany's side, then their expertise would be needed.[23]

In 1914, most everyone expected the war to be a short one. The Allied powers were strong, and

---

[21] "PEF Annual III: The Wilderness of Zin (revised 3rd edition)," *The Palestine Exploration Fund,* accessed November 2, 2014, http://www.pef.org.uk/annuals/the-re-publication-of-the-wilderness-of-zin-pef-annual-iii-by-cl-woolley-and-te-lawrence.
[22] Korda, *Hero,* 225.
[23] Anderson, *Lawrence in Arabia,* 71.

Britain boasted a royal navy that was the strongest in the world. By September 1914, however, it was increasingly clear that the war would be neither short nor bloodless. Within weeks, both sides had already suffered thousands of deaths and casualties, and it was becoming abundantly clear that his was not going to be the short war that both sides had predicted it would be.

Lawrence's frustration at being unable to join the war efforts was apparent in his writings at that time. "I am writing a learned work on Moses and his wanderings. I have a horrible fear that the Turks do not intend to go to war," he wrote in a letter to a friend dated September 18.[24] To make matters worse for Lawrence, in early October, Woolley succeeded in getting a commission in the Royal Artillery and was sent to France. No doubt his success when compared to that of Lawrence was due to the fact that Woolley was a great deal taller than Lawrence.[25] Lawrence was left to finish writing *The Wilderness of Zin* alone.

Chapter 3: The Start of Lawrence's Military Career

---

[24] Ibid., 72.
[25] Korda, *Hero,* 230.

Pictures of Lawrence during the war

"Do not try to do too much with your own hands. Better the Arabs do it tolerably than that you do it perfectly. It is their war, and you are to help them, not to win it for them. Actually, also, under the very odd conditions of Arabia, your practical work will not be as good as, perhaps, you think it is." – Lawrence of Arabia's advice to officers

The Middle East at the outbreak of the war was of secondary importance to all the great powers. As Lawrence himself called it, the region was "a sideshow of a sideshow."[26] Oil had not been discovered in Arabia, and the vast stretch of desert held little geopolitical or economic importance when compared to the cities of Europe that were under direct threat by enemy countries. As a result, Britain and many other countries sent whoever they could spare from the truly important battlefields to the Middle East, and often, this meant that inexperienced and insufficiently trained young officers were sent to the distant desert lands, including Lawrence.

Lawrence's patience finally paid off when Hogarth was able to secure him a post with the Geographical Section of the General Staff (GSGS) as a civilian. Lawrence had positive and negative experiences in this position. Though his superiors were greatly satisfied with his work and dedication, many of his colleagues were not; a stubborn and self-confident man like

---

[26] Anderson, *Lawrence in Arabia*, 4.

Lawrence, who held unorthodox views but wore no uniform in a position of some status and command, led to disgruntlement in the GSGS. By the end of October 1914, Lawrence was commissioned as a "Temporary 2nd Lieutenant-Interpreter," just one week before the Allied powers declared war on the Ottoman Empire.[27]

Following Turkey's entry into the war on the side of Germany and Austria-Hungary, Lawrence fully expected to be transferred to Cairo. His language skills, as well as his experience as a surveyor and his personal knowledge of the region gained from his travels through Palestine, Lebanon, Syria, and Turkey, made Lawrence an ideal, if not perfect, candidate. Stewart Newcombe was recalled from France to head up a new military intelligence unit in Cairo, and unsurprisingly, Newcombe immediately called on both Lawrence and Leonard Woolley to join it. Lawrence was no doubt excited to finally leave his desk and travel closer to where the action was.

In December 1914, Lawrence traveled with Newcombe to Cairo. At age 26, he was the youngest member of the Military Intelligence Department – Newcombe, its director, was 34, and Leonard Woolley was 32. Though Lawrence complained in letters to friends that he was the "bottle-washer and office boy pencil-sharpener and pen wiper," he was in truth far more than that.[28] He drew maps, tracked the location of Turkish regiments, and monitored the size, leadership, and weapons strength of these regiments.

Lawrence had never received military training, so he was unfamiliar with the massive bureaucratic structure that comprised the military, or its policies and culture. As he had struggled to "fit in" in the GSGS, Lawrence also struggled to adapt to an environment in which his thoughts and strategies were not immediately heard and respected as they had been in academia. Lawrence realized that he could not make suggestions, as these would not be heard in his position at the bottom of the massive military and governmental bureaucracies; he had to have a definitive plan. Lawrence thus began pondering how Turkey might fall, and how he could formulate a plan to achieve this.

Most in the British military and government assumed everyone who wore a Turkish uniform was Turkish. They knew nothing about the sheer diversity of the population – the ethnic, religious, cultural, and linguistic divisions and conflicts that were present in the Ottoman Empire. But Lawrence was acutely aware of the diversity, and he began to believe that the local Arabs, Kurds, and other minorities would be important players, and Arab nationalism would be the key in running the Turks out of the region. At the same time, Lawrence was also unaware of the status of the various groups of Arab nationalists, such as how many there were or how strong they were. Furthermore, the British had long been hesitant about any encouragement of Arab nationalism; just like the British government in India condemned Arab nationalism since it might spread to Indian Muslims, the authorities in the British protectorate of Egypt were reluctant to

---

[27] Korda, *Hero*, 231.
[28] Harold Orlans, *T.E. Lawrence: Biography of a Broken Hero* (London: McFarland, 2002), 25.

encourage a movement that might spark a protest against British rule in Egypt. Nonetheless, Lawrence knew early on that these Arab nationalist groups, and the diversity of Arabia, would play a key role in defeating the Ottoman Empire.

At the same time, Lawrence was well aware that the Allies could not defeat Turkey through regular warfare, and that they needed an irregular strategy. Constantinople could not be reached by land, and Lawrence identified the one place – the Gulf of Alexandretta (now Iskenderun) in northwest Syria – where the Empire was most vulnerable. He pushed for an attack on Alexandretta and in January 1915 sent a proposal to London, which was met with positive approval. Though Lawrence would later claim that the Alexandretta scheme "was, from beginning to end, my invention, put forward necessarily through my chiefs," in truth, the idea had been canvassed well before Lawrence's arrival in Cairo.[29] Still, he certainly gave the plan new momentum, as he had identified the political potential of the Alexandretta scheme when others only saw the military potential. Lawrence wrote in a military intelligence memorandum on January 5, 1915 that pushed for this scheme: "We have been informed from two good sources that the Germans in command in Syria dread nothing so much as a landing by us in the north of Syria—they say themselves that this would be followed by a general defection of their Arab troops. There is no doubt that this fear is well founded, and that a general Arab revolt, directed by the Pan-Arab military league, would be the immediate result of our occupation of Alexandretta."[30]

Any country in wartime risks great resentment and discontent among its people as the war drags on, and while this was true for all the Allied and Central countries, it was especially so for Turkey, whose empire was a chaotic amalgamation of various ethnicities, religions, and cultures. Any action that Turkey took won the support of some groups but sparked opposition from others. When Turkish leaders called for jihad against their enemies, pious Muslim youth rallied around the call, but Turkey's non-Muslim populations were terrified by it. When the government attempted to use Turkish nationalism as a way to boost morale, the Arab, Kurdish, and other ethnic populations resisted. Though most of these divergent groups were geographically separated – some geographic areas were distinctly Arab, while other areas were distinctly Turkish – there was one city where various sects, ethnic groups, and cultures lived together: Alexandretta. Using the city's divisions, Lawrence realized that a siege on Alexandretta would lead to greater divisions and discontent within the Ottoman Empire, and he was convinced that the British landing in Alexandretta would cause immediate revolts and uprisings of the people against their Turkish rulers.

The Alexandretta scheme was adopted but then dropped due to French opposition. In the meantime, Lawrence experienced personal shock when he learned that his youngest brother Frank was killed in action on the Western Front in May 1915. Letters home with news of Frank's

---

[29] Orlans, *T.E. Lawrence: Biography of a Broken Hero*, 26.
[30] Anderson, *Lawrence in Arabia*, 99.

death that were sent to Lawrence indicate his typical stoicism and starkness; Lawrence openly disapproved of his family's mourning Frank, as "to die for one's country is a sort of privilege."[31] This serves as another example of Lawrence's complex character and personality, and his lifelong effort to cut himself away from emotions and from weakness. There is no doubt, however, that Lawrence was immensely shocked by Frank's death, and his second younger brother Will's death several months later in October 1915. "They were both younger…and it doesn't seem right, somehow, that I should go on living peacefully in Cairo," he wrote to a friend.[32]

In March 1916, Lawrence and the head of naval intelligence in Mesopotamia, Aubrey Herbert, were sent to Mesopotamia on a secret mission organized by the most senior authorities in London and Cairo. The secret mission had two purposes. The urgent one was to attempt to buy the release of General Townshend and his forces by offering a £1 million bribe to the Turkish General who was besieging Townshend and his 17,000 troops outside Kut in Mesopotamia. The more hidden purpose of this mission was to observe the political and social conditions there in Mesopotamia, in order to assess the feasibility of spurring an Arab uprising in the region. The mission failed miserably when the bribe was rejected and scornfully broadcasted to world media.[33]

Chapter 4: The Start of the Arab Revolt

"It seemed that rebellion must have an unassailable base, something guarded not merely from attack, but from the fear of it: such a base as we had in the Red Sea Parts, the desert, or in the minds of the men we converted to our creed. It must have a sophisticated alien enemy, in the form of a disciplined army of occupation too small to fulfil the doctrine of acreage: too few to adjust number to space, in order to dominate the whole area effectively from fortified posts. It must have a friendly population, not actively friendly, but sympathetic to the point of not betraying rebel movements to the enemy. Rebellions can be made by 2 per cent. active in a striking force, and 98 per cent. passively sympathetic. The few active rebels must have the qualities of speed and endurance, ubiquity and independence of arteries of supply. They must have the technical equipment to destroy or paralyse the enemy's organized communications, for irregular war is fairly Willisen's definition of strategy, 'the study of communication' in its extreme degree, of attack where the enemy is not. " – Lawrence of Arabia

On June 5, 1916, Sharif Hussein bin Ali of Mecca started the Arab Revolt against the Ottoman Empire when forces commanded by Hussein's sons attacked a Turkish garrison at Medina in an attempt to seize the railway station there.[34] Several days later, Sharif Hussein publicly and officially proclaimed the start of the revolt on June 10 in Mecca, where he successfully led his forces there to seize the city. The revolt took the world by surprise, to the extent that even the

---

[31] Korda, *Hero,* 242.
[32] Orlans, *T.E. Lawrence,* 26.
[33] Ibid., 26-27.
[34] "The Ottoman Empire: Page 8 – The Arab Revolt, 1916-18)," *NZ History,* accessed November 5, 2014, http://www.nzhistory.net.nz/war/ottoman-empire/arab-revolt.

British in Cairo, who had been sending military aid to Hussein's forces in the Hejaz throughout 1915, were surprised that Hussein would actually lead his forces to revolt.

Sharif Hussein bin Ali

Sharif Hussein, born in 1853 as Hussein bin Ali, was a well-respected Hashemite who claimed direct descent from the Prophet Muhammad. He was the Sharif (steward) and Emir (ruler) of the holy city of Mecca by 1908, and as a result of holding such a widely respected position, Hussein had great influence over a vast population of Arabs in Arabia.[35] Lawrence was more or less aware that there had been negotiations taking place between the British and Hussein, and thanks to Hussein's network of influence, British authorities were keen on keeping him on their side.

---

[35] "King Hussein," *PBS,* accessed November 5, 2014, http://www.pbs.org/lawrenceofarabia/players/hussein.html.

British Secretary of State for War, Lord Herbert Kitchener, personally appealed to Hussein for his allegiance in the conflict. Throughout 1915, Hussein and the British exchanged many letters, with Hussein laying out his terms. There was one thing he absolutely required – Arab independence – and the two sides differed on what this meant and how it could be implemented. Kitchener eventually agreed to the idea of an "Arab nation," and he offered political recognition for such a nation in return for assurances of assistance in the war effort against the Turks.

At the same time, Hussein was engaging in talks with the Turks throughout his negotiation with the British. In the end, he chose to support the Allied cause, since he ultimately deemed that siding with the British would most likely allow him to deliver his goal of Arab independence.[36] He hinted to the British that with enough external support and promises from Britain that it would stay out of internal Arabian affairs, he might lead his "immediate followers into revolt."[37] To this, Kitchener eagerly responded that "Great Britain will guarantee the independence, rights and privileges of the Sherifate against all foreign aggression, in particular that of the Ottomans. Till now we have defended and befriended Islam in the person of the Turks…henceforward it shall be in that of the noble Arab."[38] This would be one of many promises that Britain's imperialist culture made and then later broke.

---

[36] James Schneider, *Guerilla Leader: T.E. Lawrence and the Arab Revolt* (London: Random House, 2011), 24.
[37] Anderson, *Lawrence in Arabia*, 116.
[38] Ibid., 117.

Kitchener

Little known was that an agreement named the Sykes-Picot Agreement had been signed in May 1916. In this secret deal, whose existence was known to very few, Britain and France had agreed to divide the Ottoman Empire's Middle Eastern territories into their own zones of influence should the Ottoman Empire fall. The publication of this agreement a year later would cause massive controversy among those fighting for the Arab Revolt, but neither Sharif Hussein nor Lawrence had any knowledge of the Sykes-Picot Agreement before the Arab Revolt began. Making conflicting promises and double dealing were part of the war strategy for Britain and for many other countries fighting in the war, a strategy that Lawrence resented. On the other hand, if exaggerated words and unsupportable promises could bring the war to an end and save the lives of millions of young Britons, then why shouldn't the British try to do everything in their power? Thus, when Britain promised "independence" to Sharif Hussein, the definition of what "independence" meant was kept vague. This was still the early 1900s, when imperialism and colonialism were a great part of global politics, so independence to the Europeans thus did not mean self-independence, like Sharif Hussein thought it did, but governing from a distance through the installation of a puppet ruler. From the start, Britain was imagining "independence" to mean "suzerainty" or "protectorate," much as Egypt was at this time, but it also made no effort to ensure that the meaning was clear for Sharif Hussein.

By the time the revolt began, Lawrence had returned to Cairo from the failed secret mission to Mesopotamia with Aubrey Herbert. Hearing about the revolt, he suddenly found his intelligence work mundane. As the revolt began to stagnate after its initial burst of success, Lawrence followed it into the fall of 1916 with increased frustration and concern. He decided to go on leave to join a British intelligence and liaison mission to the Hejaz, headed by Ronald Storrs, who was the Oriental Secretary in Cairo at the time. On this mission, Lawrence was able to meet with Sharif Hussein's four sons, who themselves would play key roles in the Arab Revolt: Ali, Faisal, Abdullah, and Zeid.[39]

Lawrence first met Abdullah when he joined Storrs's meeting with Abdullah in Jeddah. Abdullah was well known among the British as his father's most trusted son; if Sharif Hussein was the spiritual leader of the revolt, Abdullah was its operational leader, akin to a field marshal. Throughout the meeting, Lawrence observed Abdullah, and at the end, he concluded that Abdullah was too ambitious and too much of a politician to be an effective military strategist and leader. Lawrence thus decided that what the revolt was lacking, and the reason behind the revolt's stagnation, was true leadership, "not intellect, nor judgment, nor political wisdom, but the flame of enthusiasm that would set the desert on fire."[40] To Lawrence, Abdullah was too calculating, too balanced, and too cool to provide such fiery leadership to the revolt that Lawrence felt was necessary.

---

[39] "Outline Chronology: 1916," *T.E. Lawrence Studies,* accessed November 5, 2014, http://www.telstudies.org/biography/chron_1916.shtml.
[40] Anderson, *Lawrence in Arabia,* 196.

Abdullah

The next morning, Lawrence presented a proposal to Abdullah. What the revolt was lacking was reliable information, particularly about what was actually taking place on the ground. They needed an objective observer, one who was knowledgeable of the politics of the region but also able to remain purely objective. He raised the example of the problems another son of Sharif Hussein's, Faisal, was facing in the northern mountains near the port town of Rabegh. Faisal was being bombarded by Turkish planes, and logistical problems were preventing him from gaining access to key supplies. More objective information on the ground could solve these kind of problems, he said. Then, Lawrence suggested that he be the man to carry out this mission. Abdullah immediately agreed.[41]

Though Abdullah initially suggested that Faisal come to Lawrence so that the two may meet, Lawrence politely refused and instead stated that he would like to go to Faisal, for as he crossed the lands of Arabia, he would be able to see and assess the situation inland for himself. Though non-Muslims were strictly discouraged from traveling across the inlands of Arabia, Abdullah finally relented, under the condition that Lawrence meet with Sharif Hussein's eldest son, Ali, first in Rabegh. If Ali saw Lawrence fit to continue his travels, Abdullah stated that Ali would

---
[41] Ibid., 200.

arrange for Lawrence to make the rest of the journey to Faisal.[42]

Lawrence thus met Ali and Zeid – the youngest son of Sharif Hussein – in Rabegh. Lawrence took an immediate liking to Ali, in whom he saw great leadership potential. Ali approved of Lawrence as well, but he voiced his concerns about Lawrence's planned hundred-mile trek to where Faisal's camp lay, because parts of the trip would take Lawrence through territories controlled by tribes hostile to the Arab Revolt. Undeterred, Lawrence soon headed out on his journey with two of Ali's most trusted lieutenants, and despite the discomfort he experienced from traveling a long distance by camel, Lawrence was able to make detailed notes of the terrain he was crossing. He arrived at Faisal's camp in the early afternoon of October 23.[43]

---

[42] Ibid., 200-202.
[43] Ibid., 24.

Ali

Lawrence described his initial impression of Faisal, the man he hoped would become the true leader of the Arab Revolt, as such: "He was a man of moods…flickering between glory and despair, and just now dead tired. He looked years older than thirty-one, and his dark, appealing eyes, set a little sloping in his face, were bloodshot, and his hollow cheeks deeply lined and puckered with reflection. His nature grudged thinking, for it crippled his speed in action: the labour of it shriveled his features into swift lines of pain. In appearance he was tall, graceful and vigorous, with the most beautiful gait, and a royal dignity of head and shoulders. Of course he knew it, and a great part of his public expression was by sign and gesture."[44]

Faisal

In addition to Faisal's character, Lawrence was able to walk through the camp and interact with the men that made up Faisal's force. He was surprised to find the great number of different tribes that were represented in this camp; Arabian politics was largely based on clan and tribal politics, and Lawrence knew it took great leadership skills and shrewdness to amass this many men from this many tribes. Lawrence left the camp convinced that Faisal was the leader of the revolt he had been seeking.

Thus began Lawrence's struggle to convince his British superiors that Faisal was the man, and not Abdullah, while also persuading them to scale back any British military presence in Arabia. Obviously, Lawrence knew nothing of the Sykes-Picot Agreement, as only a handful of the most senior British and French officials knew of the agreement, so he pushed for the British to show that they meant to honor their agreement of supporting the post-war creation of an "Arab nation." To do this, the British must not deploy troops to Arabia, for Faisal was already distrustful that the British meant to commandeer his efforts once the deed of running out the Turks was done. "They are our very good friends while we respect their independence," Lawrence argued in a

---

[44] T.E. Lawrence, *Seven Pillars of Wisdom: A Triumph* (New York: Knopf Doubleday Publishing Group, 2013), 96-98.

memorandum. "They are deeply grateful for the help we have given them, but they fear lest we may make it a claim upon them afterwards. We have appropriated too many Moslem countries for them to have any real trust in our disinterestedness and they are terribly afraid of an English occupation of Hejaz."[45] It was soon decided that a British military advisor should accompany Faisal, and the man for this job was Lawrence. By the end of the year, Lawrence was back at Faisal's camp. When Faisal gifted him with Arab clothes, fit for camel riding, Lawrence gladly accepted the white silk robes.

On January 3, 1917, Lawrence set off on his first desert raid with 35 other tribesmen, and the raid ultimately ended in success when Lawrence and his men were able to capture two Turks

---

[45] Anderson, *Lawrence of Arabia*, 223.

near a Turkish encampment and take them back for questioning. However, on this raid, Lawrence was forced to act as the military commander of his band when one of the tribesmen, Hamed, murdered another. The two tribesmen were from different tribes and had been feuding, and the relatives of the murdered man demanded blood for blood, so to prevent a blood feud from breaking out, Lawrence could think of no other way but to personally execute Hamed himself. The experience would haunt him forever, as he wrote, "[A]fterwards, the wakeful night dragged over me, till, hours before dawn, I had the men up and made them load…They had to lift me into the saddle."[46]

Lawrence had long worked hard to be "unlike a soldier," to not be confined to military protocol and responsibility, and to be allowed to simply work on his projects freely. When he was selected to be the British representative and advisor to Faisal, he initially resisted, as he did not have the training, nor the mindset, required of a commander to direct the Arab war. But he was sternly told that Faisal must be linked to the British, and someone with proper experience and expertise must go and do so. "So I had to go," Lawrence wrote in his autobiography, *Seven Pillars of Wisdom*: "Leaving to others the *Arab Bulletin*[47] I had founded, the maps I wished to draw, and the file of war-changes of the Turkish Army, all fascinating activities in which my training helped me, to take up a role for which I felt no inclination."[48] Though this sullenness dissipated as he joined Faisal in his campaign across Arabia, doubts about his military capacity and abilities would remain. "As our revolt succeeded, onlookers have praised its leadership: but behind the scenes lay all the vices of amateur control, experimental councils, divisions, whimsicality."[49]

The execution of Hamed was Lawrence's first true insertion into the role of a commanding officer, and of a soldier. It served as his wake-up call that he was no longer in the mapping room back in Cairo, tracking the Turkish forces' strength and playing strategist behind-the-scenes. He was now on the ground, in the midst of hundreds of Arab fighters from dozens of different tribes, leading a war for the independence of Arabia.

Chapter 5: The Capture of Aqaba

"Rebels, especially successful rebels, were of necessity bad subjects and worse governors." – Lawrence of Arabia

Faisal and Lawrence established an immediate rapport, and Lawrence began sharing his thoughts and plans with his newly made friend and hopeful leader of the Arab Revolt. Instead of heading to Medina to attempt to capture the city once more, Lawrence persuaded Faisal to

---

[46] Lawrence, *Seven Pillars of Wisdom,* 181.
[47] The *Arab Bulletin* was a clandestine and secretive series of reports and documents that were circulated by the Arab Bureau in Cairo, of which Lawrence was part of. It reached only the highest levels of the British government and military structure.
[48] Ibid., 114.
[49] Ibid.

engage in guerilla warfare, attacking supply and rail lines and disrupting the Turks' line of communications. This not only disrupted Turkish operations but also forced the Turks to diffuse their forces along supply and communication routes, preventing them from effectively fighting against the regular forces under the command of the British General Edward Allenby.[50] Lawrence's relationship with Faisal deepened with every victory, and Faisal's Arab Northern Army was swiftly becoming the main beneficiary of British aid and support.[51]

Allenby

Lawrence then brought a bold plan to Faisal's attention: the capture of a port. A major port under the Arabs' control would allow for an easier time receiving arms and supplies from the British. Lawrence thus suggested that Faisal's forces make their way across the desert and attack Aqaba (now part of Jordan) by land. Aqaba was one of the most key and strategic ports in the region, as it was the ideal staging ground to organize attacks into southern Palestine and for

---

[50] "TE Lawrence (1888-1935)," *BBC*, accessed November 5, 2014, http://www.bbc.co.uk/history/historic_figures/lawrence_te.shtml.
[51] Murphy, *The Arab Revolt 1916-1918*, 36.

launching raids along the Hejaz rail line, which was the lifeline of the Turkish forces occupying Medina. In April 1917, Lawrence formulated with Faisal a plan to capture Aqaba.[52] Their plan was a land attack, as most of Aqaba's defenses were concentrated on the possibility of a sea attack. Lawrence went off to make contact with Auda Abu Tayi, the chief of the powerful Bedouin tribal confederation of northern Arabi. With money, Lawrence was able to secure Abu Tayi's allegiance, despite the fact that Abu Tayi had been on the side of the Ottomans prior to this.[53] In addition, Lawrence and Faisal secured the loyalty and cooperation of various other tribes of the region, further burgeoning their strength.

On July 2, 1917, Lawrence's forces began their assault on Aqaba with an attack on Aba El Lissan, an outpost outside of Aqaba. Though initial attempts seemed unsuccessful, Abu Tayi led a mounted charge against Turkish forces, quickly leading to the defeat of the terrified Turkish forces.[54] Lawrence later recalled of this battle in *Seven Pillars*: "We kicked our camels furiously to the edge, to see our fifty horsemen coming down the last slope into the main valley like a runaway, at full gallop, shooting from the saddle. As we watched, two or three went down, but the rest thundered forward at marvelous speed, and the Turkish infantry, huddled together under the cliff ready to cut their desperate way out towards Maan, in the first dusk began to sway in and out, and finally broke before the rush, adding their flight to Auda's charge."[55] On his prized camel, named Namaa, Lawrence raced down to join the forces sweeping toward the shrieking Turkish forces. Only two Arab fighters were killed in the attack, but hundreds of Turkish soldiers lay dead or dying.[56] By July 6, 1917, Aqaba was declared to be under the control of Faisal.

With the successful capture of Aqaba, Lawrence was able to secure his place as a chief adviser to Faisal, as well as prove himself in the eyes of British senior authorities. Aqaba was transformed into a new base for Faisal's forces, as well as an important base for raids into northern Syria. Faisal thus subsequently placed himself under the command of the British General Allenby, who was commanding Palestine. Allenby, recognizing the great strength and influence Faisal and his forces could provide, supplied Faisal's forces with weapons, ammunition, and funds.

The attack on Aqaba was also the first slaughter Lawrence had ever witnessed. "The dead men looked wonderfully beautiful," Lawrence recalled as he viewed the littered dead bodies after the battle.[57] One must take note that though Lawrence was a scholar well versed in military history and tactics, he had never received military training. The deaths he witnessed in Aqaba were significant, as they made him redefine his purpose and mission.

---

[52] Spencer C. Tucker, *The Encyclopedia of World War I* (Santa Barbara: ABC-CLIO, 2005), 115.
[53] Fromkin, *A Peace to End All Peace*, 309.
[54] "The Taking of Akaba," *Clio Visualizing History,* accessed November 5, 2014, http://www.cliohistory.org/thomas-lawrence/akaba/.
[55] Lawrence, *Seven Pillars of Wisdom,* 303.
[56] Anderson, *Lawrence in Arabia,* 335.
[57] Anthony Nutting, *Lawrence of Arabia: The Man and the Motive* (New York: Signet, 1961), 74.

Chapter 6: The End of the War

"With hindsight, it is easy to see why a slim, self-effacing Englishman named Thomas Edward Lawrence became one of this century's most ballyhooed celebrities. Out of the appalling carnage of World War I — the mud-caked anonymity of the trenches, the hail of mechanized death that spewed from machine guns and fell from airplanes — there emerged a lone Romantic, framed heroically against the clean desert sands of Arabia." – Paul Gray

The capture of Aqaba proved to be one of the most important events in the course of the Arab Revolt. With the port seized, the British were able to send funds, weapons, and supplies directly to the Arab forces, and Aqaba was transformed into a military base, becoming the conduit of information, arms, and money for the Arab and British forces. Furthermore, the capture of Aqaba was also a great morale booster for the Arabs, and it catapulted the Arab Revolt into a force to be reckoned with. As the Arab Revolt grew more successful, and as its success became more definite, more tribes began to join it. Lawrence recalled, "After the capture of Aqaba...things changed so much that I was no longer a witness of the Revolt, but a protagonist in the Revolt."[58] He was being modest, however, as he continued to command the Arab army to victories. In January 1918, at the Battle of Tafileh, Lawrence and Faisal led their forces to another seizure of a key location. The battle was described as a "brilliant feat of arms," and Lawrence was awarded the Distinguished Service Order by the British government and promoted to Lieutenant-Colonel.[59] By 1918, Turkish authorities were offering a sizeable reward of £15,000 for Lawrence's head.[60]

One unexpected event that threatened the solidarity of Lawrence's relations with Faisal and his army was the exposure of the existence of the Sykes-Picot Agreement in 1917. Following the November 1917 Bolshevik Revolution in Russia, the Communists led by Vladimir Lenin discovered a copy of the agreement in the government archives. Russia had received a copy of the agreement from the British and the French because Russia was promised spheres of influence in Turkish Armenia and northern Kurdistan.[61] The Bolsheviks published the copy of the agreement in their national newspapers – the *Izvestia* and *Pravada* – on November 23, 1917, and the *Manchester Guardian* subsequently printed it on November 26, 1917.[62] The Sykes-Picot Agreement understandably startled Faisal and his Arab fighters. Lawrence and all of the other British officers fighting alongside the Arabs were also equally appalled. An international outrage ensued after the publication of the agreement – Britain had only just signed the Balfour Declaration three weeks earlier, which promised British support for a Jewish homeland in

---

[58] O'Brien Browne, "T.E. Lawrence: The Enigmatic Lawrence of Arabia," *Military History,* October 2003, http://www.historynet.com/te-lawrence-the-enigmatic-lawrence-of-arabia.htm.
[59] Patrick Richard Carstens, *The Encyclopædia of Egypt during the Reign of the Mehemet Ali Dynasty 1798-1952: The People, Places and Events that Shaped Nineteenth Century Egypt and its Sphere of Influence* (Victoria, BC: Friesen Press, 2104), 412.
[60] Mack, *A Prince of Our Disorder,* 158.
[61] "The Sykes-Picot Agreement of 1916," *History Learning Site,* accessed November 5, 2014, http://www.historylearningsite.co.uk/sykes_picot_agreement.htm.
[62] "Jordan-Syria Boundary," *International Boundary Study* no. 94 (Office of the Geographer, Bureau of Intelligence and Research, 1969), 9.

Palestine – and the exposure of the treaty greatly embarrassed the Allied powers. The Agreement also directly contradicted the McMahon-Hussein Correspondence[63], in which Henry McMahon, the British High Commissioner in Egypt, promised British recognition of Arab independence in return for an Arab revolt in alliance with the Allied powers and against the Ottoman Empire.[64]

After the exposure of what was once a secretive Sykes-Picot Agreement, doubts and anxiety regarding the Allied powers' true intentions spread across the Arab forces. For some time, the disclosure of the treaty hurt the British position among the Arabs, particularly that of Lawrence, but he was still able to persuade Faisal, whom he now considered a good friend, that he could be trusted. Lawrence explained, "I…had convinced him that his escape [from this double dealing] was to help the British so much that after peace they would not be able, for shame, to shoot him down in its [Arab independence's] fulfillment…I begged him to trust not in our promises, like his father, but in his own strong performance."[65] In the end, however reluctantly, Faisal was persuaded, and he vowed continued cooperation with the British.

Ever the soldier, Faisal was quick to discard uncertainties and lumber on for the goal of Arab freedom, but in contrast, Lawrence could not get over the shock of the secret British betrayal that had run so counter to what he had been fighting to accomplish. He plunged into a deep depression, of which he later wrote, "[I]n revenge, I vowed to make the Arab Revolt the engine of its own success…to lead it madly in the final victory that expediency should counsel to the Powers a fair settlement of the Arabs' moral claims."[66]

Another incident that occurred in November 1917 that impacted Lawrence greatly was Lawrence's capture and night of torture in the city of Dera'a. During a reconnaissance mission to Dera'a, then occupied by Turkish forces, Lawrence and three Arab companions were stopped by Turkish officers. Though his companions were allowed to go on their way, Lawrence was suspected of being a Turkish army deserter and was taken in to see the *bey* (chief) of the Turkish armed forces in Dera'a. There, he experienced brutal physical assault (possibly of a sexual nature) at the hands of the *bey* and his guardsmen.[67]

Lawrence dedicated a full chapter in his *Seven Pillars of Wisdom* to this incident at Dera'a, and the excruciating torture that he experienced was recounted in great literary detail. He wrote that the torture ended when he was "completely broken," but he managed to escape from the hands of the Turks by putting on a "suit of shoddy clothes" that he found in the room he was being kept in and climbing out a window. He wrote that he was then able to negotiate a ride from a passing

---

[63] The McMahon-Hussein Correspondence (also known as the Hussein-McMahon Correspondence) is the name of the series of letters that were exchanged between July 1915 and January 1916 between Sir Henry McMahon, the British High Commissioner in Egypt, and Sharif Hussein, that guaranteed British support for an Arab state following the fall of the Ottoman Empire.
[64] Ibid.
[65] Lawrence, *Seven Pillars of Wisdom*, 555.
[66] Browne, "T.E. Lawrence: The Enigmatic Lawrence of Arabia."
[67] Anderson, *Lawrence in Arabia*, 398-400.

camel-borne merchant to a nearby village where he had arranged to rendezvous with the companions he was separated from.[68]

Biographers and historians have fervently argued about the events of that day. The biggest unanswered question is whether Lawrence was sexually assaulted, and the only information that can be considered to answer this question is Lawrence's own account in *Seven Pillars of Wisdom* – there exist no other accounts of this day that could clarify what truly happened. However, despite writing about the physical torture in lurid detail, Lawrence kept the *bey*'s sexual intentions vague. According to biographer Scott Anderson, most Lawrence biographers have concluded that the Dera'a incident simply could not have happened as described, and some have said that it did not even occur at all. Anyone who received torture as severe as what Lawrence described he experienced would undoubtedly be unable to climb out of the window he was being kept in and simply walk out of the city. Years later, some of Lawrence's comrades and companions were questioned about this incident, but none knew anything about it, and several would recall that though Lawrence seemed preoccupied upon his return from the mission to Dera'a, he had no cuts, bruises, or wounds that would indicate he received any kind of torture.[69]

Regardless of what actually happened, Dera'a did change Lawrence. Lawrence wrote about "how in Dera'a that night the citadel of my integrity had been irrevocably lost" in *Seven Pillars of Wisdom*.[70] This and the exposure of the Sykes-Picot Agreement burdened Lawrence greatly. Though he continued along with Faisal's army, visiting one Bedouin camp after another and trying to get various tribes to join the cause of the Arab Revolt, the guilt continued to bring Lawrence's spirits down. The Arab fighters saw him as the British representative on the ground, and they thus sought promises and assurances from him. Lawrence recounted in *Seven Pillars*, "I had to join the conspiracy, and, for what my word was worth, assured the men of their reward. In our two years' partnership under fire they grew accustomed to believing me and to think my Government, like myself, sincere. In this hope they performed some fine things, but of course, instead of being proud of what we did together, I was continually and bitterly ashamed. It was evident from the beginning that if we won the war these promises would be dead paper, and had I been an honest adviser of the Arabs I would have advised them to go home and not risk their lives fighting for such stuff."[71]

Regardless of Lawrence's rising anxiety, the war continued on. After a series of battles fought and won by General Edmund Allenby, who was heading the British Empire's Egyptian Expeditionary Force (EEF), British forces marched into Jerusalem on December 11, 1917 to secure the city. Allenby invited Lawrence to enter the city with him on foot, which Lawrence accepted delightedly. For Lawrence, the capture of Jerusalem was one of "the supreme moments of the war."[72]

---

[68] Lawrence, *Seven Pillars of Wisdom*, 447.
[69] Anderson, *Lawrence in Arabia*, 400-401.
[70] Lawrence, *Seven Pillars of Wisdom*, 447.
[71] Ibid., 25-26.

Lawrence, Abdullah, and others in Jerusalem

All eyes now turned to Syria, and General Allenby was tasked with the taking of Damascus. Though Lawrence had intended to ask for his removal from his position, he was called upon yet again because Faisal's forces would play a crucial role in a Syria offensive. "There was no

---

[72] Lawrence, *Seven Pillars of Wisdom,* 453.

escape for me," he recalled. "I must take up again my mantle of fraud in the East."[73] Lawrence continued to try to convince his superiors that an independent Arab state was in the interest of Britain.

Throughout 1918, Allenby focused all his strengths on Damascus, using every resource he had available. He tasked Faisal's Northern Arab Army with continuing their tactics of guerilla warfare, cutting railway and communication lines and conducting raids against the Turks to disrupt their operations. Lawrence, Faisal, and their forces made their way north toward Damascus, and as they did so, their army gained in strength as more and more tribesmen joined Faisal's army with the victory of the Arab army seeming near.

It was on their trek to Damascus that Lawrence experienced another disturbing incident that would scar him for the rest of his life. In September 1918, Faisal's army won a battle against a brigade of Turkish, Austrian, and German troops near the village of Tafas, which the Turks had plundered during their retreat. After finding evidence of enemy atrocities against the Arab residents of Tafas, Faisal's forces took revenge on the surrendered Turkish and German prisoners by murdering them in cold blood. Whether the Turks actually committed atrocities, and what role Lawrence had in either killing or spurring the killing of the prisoners of war, remain topics of great discussion and debate.[74] Lawrence wrote of the events in Tafas in *Seven Pillars of Wisdom*, "In a madness born of the horror of Tafas we killed and killed, even blowing in the heads of the fallen and of the animals; as though their death and running blood could slake our agony."[75]

Ever anxious to assure Arab independence, Lawrence aimed to be the first into Damascus so that Faisal's forces could claim the capture of the city and establish their authority for the inevitable peace talks that would follow. However, he was slightly delayed, so he arrived several hours after the city's formal surrender on October 1, 1918. The joy he felt for the fall of Damascus was brief, because when Lawrence entered the city hall, he was frustrated to find Damascus leaders and Bedouin leaders in the midst of a heated argument, all of them armed. Old grudges and family feuds were boiling over, and a violent fight broke out.[76] Nonetheless, Lawrence intervened, and he played a vital role in the eventual establishment of a provisional government in Syria led by Faisal.

On October 3, 1918, when both Allenby and Faisal arrived in Damascus, Lawrence acted as interpreter as Allenby informed Faisal that though he would recognize an Arab military administration of the occupied territory east of Jordan from Damascus to Ma'an, the British would remain in supreme command so long as the war continued. Furthermore, Allenby also reminded Faisal of the Sykes-Picot Agreement, and that the coastal regions of Syria would fall

---

[73] Anderson, *Lawrence in Arabia*, 425.
[74] "The Taking of Syria," *Clio Visualizing History,* accessed November 5, 2014, http://www.cliohistory.org/thomas-lawrence/lawrence/syria/.
[75] Lawrence, *Seven Pillars of Wisdom,* 633.
[76] Korda, *Hero,* 382.

under a French protectorate.[77] Faisal understandably reacted strongly to these words, but he ultimately accepted Allenby's promise that the matter would be fully settled at the conclusion of the war.

Lawrence left Damascus on October 4, 1918, and the war ended roughly a month later, on November 11, 1918, with Germany's signing of an armistice. By October 24, Lawrence was back home in Oxford, for the first time in a long time.[78]

Chapter 7: Lawrence's Fame and Later Years

"There is no other man I know who could have achieved what Lawrence did. As for taking undue credit for himself, my own personal experience with Lawrence is that he was utterly unconcerned whether any kudos was awarded him or not." – General Allenby

Lawrence was still intent on securing the Arab independence that he had promised Faisal and his Arab army, so he traveled to Versailles in 1919 to present his views to the British Cabinet. He also attended the 1919 Paris Peace Conference as a member of Faisal's delegation, where he again urged the fulfillment of the promise given to the Arabs. By then, however, Britain and France were already intent on partitioning the Middle East into protectorates and spheres of influence.[79]

---

[77] Mack, *A Prince of Our Disorder,* 172.
[78] Korda, *Hero,* 387.
[79] Browne, "T.E. Lawrence: The Enigmatic Lawrence of Arabia."

Faisal and Lawrence at Versailles

Faisal's provisional government in Syria did not last long. An independent United Arab Kingdom of Syria, ruled by King Faisal, was proclaimed in Damascus on March 8, 1920, but the announcement drew immediate critical responses from Britain and France. On July 24, 1920, French forces defeated Arab forces at the battle of Maysaloun and entered Damascus. The French subsequently ousted Faisal and declared Syria a French mandate.[80]

Utterly disillusioned with politics, the government, and the military, Lawrence returned to Britain. For about a year, he worked as an advisor to Winston Churchill, and he was subsequently appointed Colonial Secretary on Arab affairs and played a key role in the formation of Transjordan, but he soon felt the urge to escape public life and left the government. He subsequently refused all other offers for a career in government and instead chose to write. It was only after the end of the war and the dividing of the carcass of the fallen Ottoman Empire that Lawrence's fame would be catapulted to the point that he was considered one of the greatest heroes of the war.

As it happened, Lawrence of Arabia became a household name almost solely due to the work

---

[80] Malcolm Russell, *The Middle East and South Asia 2014* (Lanham, MD: Rowman & Littlefield, 2014), 110.

of Lowell Thomas, an American journalist who had joined Lawrence in the desert with a cameraman named Harry Chase to document the Arab Revolt. Thomas and Chase had initially been documenting events on the Western Front, but they had grown despondent while documenting the wartime brutality there. They set off for the Middle East, arriving in Jerusalem just in time to film General Allenby's historic passage through the gates of Jerusalem.[81] It was there that Thomas met T.E. Lawrence, who invited Thomas and Chase back to Faisal's desert camp.

---

[81] "Lowell Thomas," *PBS,* accessed November 8, 2014, http://www.pbs.org/lawrenceofarabia/players/thomas.html.

Lowell Thomas

According to Thomas' own account, his attention was first drawn to Lawrence when he saw him standing among a group of Arab sheiks in Jerusalem. He recalled that "it did not take long to discover that [I] had stumbled on a story in some ways more astounding [than] the 'Last Crusade' and the 'Conquest of Jerusalem.'"[82] Of Lawrence, he wrote, "Lawrence, unknown to the world, was then at the peak of his unusual career. The young Oxford archeologist, who, when war broke out, had been working at the study and excavation of the ancient cities of the Near East, now had become a sheik of the desert. With his understanding of the ways of the desert peoples of the East, he had become first a British agent and then the fiery leader arousing the Bedouin to a general revolt against their old tyrant, the Turk. And now he was leading the tribesmen of the sands against the Turkish army, raids which demoralized communications, destroyed detachments and made the Turk tear his beard with rage."[83]

The relationship between Thomas and Lawrence was of a curious nature. The two later disputed several key details that should have been facts. For example, as his fame peaked, Lawrence claimed that he had been "tricked" into being filmed and photographed by Thomas and Chase, a claim that Thomas strongly denied. According to Thomas, Lawrence had been a willing model. Lawrence claimed the shoot only lasted days, while Thomas asserted that it lasted weeks.[84] The contradicting claims and the somewhat strange relationship the two men had are likely indicative of the differences in their personalities; Thomas was a businessman and a showman at heart who knew how to find stories and market them. As such, he pounced on the idea of a white man in Arab robes riding a camel across the desert and commanding hundreds of local tribesmen to battle. Lawrence was more reticent, reserved, and modest. Though he had sought fame, when he achieved it, he shrunk away from it.

Lawrence's fame came in the summer of 1919, just as the Paris Peace Conference was underway. An estimated 1 million Britons, including the King and Queen, attended Lowell Thomas' lecture show, "With Allenby in Palestine, and Lawrence in Arabia."[85] Seeing the positive feedback in Britain, Thomas took the show on a tour around the world, modifying it for different audiences. For example, in Britain, Lawrence was referred to as "the prince of Mecca" and "the uncrowned king of Arabia," whereas in the U.S., Lawrence was described as "the George Washington of Arabia."[86] Lawrence's feats were presented all across the globe, from Australia to Southeast Asia, and from Europe to Canada.

Thomas was not a scholar, nor was he satisfied with the role of a simple journalist. As such, he knew Lawrence's story to be a good one, and he gave his greatest effort to sell the story. Thomas would go on to make $1.5 million on the show (equal to around $16 million today).[87] Though Lawrence has been criticized for cooperating with Thomas, and it does seem out of character when considering Lawrence's stoic and unemotional nature, it must be noted that Lawrence could hardly have foreseen that one documentary film would become such a global sensation. As

---

[82] "Lowell Thomas, A World Traveler and Broadcaster for 45 Years, Dead," *The New York Times,* August 30, 1981, http://www.nytimes.com/1981/08/30/obituaries/lowell-thomas-a-world-traveler-and-broadcaster-for-45-years-dead.html?pagewanted=3&pagewanted=all.
[83] Ibid.
[84] "Lowell Thomas." *PBS.*
[85] Anderson, *Lawrence in Arabia,* 486.
[86] Korda, *Hero,* 424.
[87] Ibid., 424.

a result of Thomas' work, Lawrence's name was known across the world. As the *Daily Telegraph* summed it up, "Thomas Lawrence, the archaeologist…went out to Arabia and, practically unaided, raised for the first time almost since history began a great homogeneous Arab army."[88]

Lawrence may have been stoic, but the fame undoubtedly gave him greater impetus to work on his autobiography. Using the extensive notes he took throughout the revolt, Lawrence began working on a manuscript for his autobiography in 1919, while he was still participating in the Paris Peace Conference. He claimed that his first draft was either lost or stolen at Reading Station in late 1919,[89] so he started from scratch and rewrote the manuscript over the course of a few years. Looking for more writing inspiration and a way to escape his fame, in 1922, he enlisted in the British Royal Air Force (RAF) under the assumed name of John Hume Ross. When this was discovered by the press and his superiors, he was swiftly discharged, but Lawrence remained persistent. In 1923, he joined the Royal Tank Corps (RTC) under the alias of T.E. Shaw.[90]

Biographer Michael Korda has noted that "the curious history of *Seven Pillars of Wisdom* is one of the more tangled and complicated episodes in book publishing."[91] Lawrence toyed with publishing a "boy-scout" version of the book in the U.S. that would be extremely concise, with all the controversial chapters removed. Another idea he had was to print only one copy of the book and place it in the Library of Congress to ensure copyright, or to offer the book at an exorbitant price of $200,000 or more.[92] Finally, he discarded these ideas, and in 1926, he completed *Seven Pillars of Wisdom,* which was initially only available by subscription and not for general circulation. He continued to write while serving in the RTC, and later in the RAF again, and he wrote an abridged version of the subscription *Seven Pillars* entitled *Revolt in the Desert,* which was published in 1927. Lawrence also penned a novel, *The Mint,* based on his experiences in the RAF, as well as a highly acclaimed modern translation of Homer's *Odyssey.*

The curious way in which Lawrence wrote and published his autobiography – available only by subscription first, then an abridged version published for general circulation – led to delayed appreciation for the work. Had Lawrence been willing to publish *Seven Pillars of Wisdom* in a normal way, it would certainly have been a bestseller and would have made a fortune. As writer Jennifer Speake described the work, "*Seven Pillars of Wisdom* is the account of an initiation to the desert, war, and physical suffering. Lawrence's Arabian adventure shaped, broadened, but also scarred his identity."[93] The work is not just a personal account of a revolt or objective descriptions of Arabian politics but also one that explored Lawrence's own psychological

---

[88] Ibid., 435.
[89] Ibid. 437-
[90] Browne, "T.E. Lawrence: The Enigmatic Lawrence of Arabia."
[91] Korda, *Hero,* 442.
[92] Ibid.
[93] Speake, *Literature of Travel and Exploration,* 701.

process of "going native," in his own words. Beyond wearing Arab clothing, riding a camel, and speaking Arabic, the autobiography recounts Lawrence's psychological and emotional immersion and assimilation into Arabia. It is certainly a difficult book to read through due to everything included in it. For instance, biographer Jeremy Wilson has pointed out that Lawrence started off writing the book by compiling all the intelligence reports he had written for the *Arab Bulletin* during his military days in Cairo, then decided to remedy the dryness of the content of these reports by inserting long descriptions of the people and the landscape, often touched with flowery lyricism.[94] This unevenness of the novel, together with the deluge of Arab names, places, and vocabulary that readers are flooded with, makes the book a challenge for the lay reader to get through.

Nonetheless, *Seven Pillars of Wisdom* remains one of the most well written, interesting, and starkly objective accounts of the Arab Revolt in Arabia. That some may find it exaggerated as a work of self-aggrandizement speaks to the fact that in reality, Lawrence himself was a humble, quiet, stoic man who shied away from the limelight when Lowell Thomas's show brought him the fame and glory that Lawrence thought he had wanted. When the media interviewed him, Lawrence would always bring up the valuable work and contributions of others – both British and Arab – in bringing about the Arab Revolt. Only on paper did he truly let out his pride, his fears, and his thoughts, and for this reason alone, *Seven Pillars of Wisdom* is an immensely valuable work.

---

[94] Korda, *Hero,* 441.

Chapter 8: The Death and Legacy of Lawrence

Lawrence on his motorcycle, a Brough Superior SS100 he called George V

"We shall never see his like again. His name will live in history. It will live in the annals of war...it will live in the legends of Arabia."[95] -- Winston Churchill

Despite the fame and celebrity he achieved, Lawrence suffered and fell deeper into depression. His body was wracked by illness, causing him to lose significant weight, and he suffered psychologically from the physical and mental brutality he witnessed and experienced during the Arab Revolt. On top of that, the imperialistic politics of the major powers, including his own Britain, nullified the great victory of the Arabs. Biographers tend to differ about the depth of Lawrence's depression at this time, and some believe he was experiencing something that would today be identified as "post-traumatic stress disorder (PTSD)," while others insist that though Lawrence continued to display aloof and isolationist tendencies, the notion that he locked himself into a depressed solitude is an exaggeration. In any case, it is true that Lawrence continued to suffer from bouts of nightmares, and that he preferred solitude and correspondence via letters to going out and interacting with others face-to-face. As one biographer, Scott

---

[95] Tom Cotter, *The Vincent in the Barn: Great Stories of Motorcycle Archaeology* (Motorbooks, 2009), 247.

Anderson, put it, "Despite the assertion of some biographers that this period in Lawrence's life was also highly productive and interesting, it is hard to escape the image of a sad and reclusive man, his circle of friends and acquaintances steadily dwindling to a mere handful, and many of these only maintained by the occasional quick note from Lawrence explaining why he couldn't see them."[96]

One of his few remaining passions was motorcycle riding. After he retired from the RAF in March of 1935, a mere two months later, on May 13, 1935, Lawrence was injured in a motorcycle accident near Clouds Hill, Lawrence's isolated cottage in Dorset, Southwest England. He was on his way to send a telegram when he came across two bicycling boys on a narrow road, and after swerving to avoid hitting them, he crashed and hit his head on the asphalt. He died six days later on May 19, 1935, at the age of 46, never regaining consciousness.[97]

General Allenby's tribute to Lawrence, broadcasted from London immediately after the announcement of Lawrence's death, was especially indicative of the sheer amount of respect and admiration he and many others had for Lawrence: "His co-operation was marked by the utmost loyalty and I never had anything but praise for his work, which, indeed, was invaluable throughout the campaign. He was the mainspring of the Arab movement and knew their language, their manners and their mentality. He shared with the Arabs their hardships and dangers. Among these desert raiders there was none who would not have willingly died for his chief. In fact not a few lost their lives in devotion to him and in defence of his person…He was a shy and retiring scholar, archaeologist, and philosopher swept by the tide of war in to a position undreamt of. He had a genius for leadership. Above all men he had no regard for ambition, but did his duty as he saw it…He has left to us who knew and admired him a beloved memory and to all his countrymen an example of a life well spent in service."[98]

A private funeral was held for Lawrence on May 21, 1935, attended only by his family and closest friends. It was a funeral kept as simple as anything that Lawrence could have wished. There were no flowers, and there was no mourning. Winston Churchill, who eulogized Lawrence as "one of the greatest beings alive in this time," was among the many influential attendees.

T.E. Lawrence was a complex man, with a character and motivations full of contradictions. He longed to be different, to be special, and to be remembered, but when he achieved fame, he seemed appalled by it. He sought acceptance by others, yet he was a strong individualist. Solitude and aloofness were his key traits, but he took great care to maintain correspondence with his many friends, family, and colleagues. He knew when to be modest, but many of his accounts seem exaggerated, and some possibly untrue. He was not just a scholar, an archaeologist, a writer, a soldier, or a commander, but all of these things combined.

---

[96] Anderson, *Lawrence I Arabia,* 504.
[97] Ibid., 505.
[98] "Strategist of the Desert Dies in Military Hospital: Lord Allenby's Tribute – 'Valued Comrade,'" *The Guardian,* May 19, 1935, http://www.theguardian.com/theguardian/1935/may/19/fromthearchive.

Either way, T.E. Lawrence's legacy has proven to be timeless. Lawrence's name is repeatedly evoked at political conventions, military meetings, and diplomatic conferences alike, nearly a century after the revolt he helped to lead. His strategy of "irregular warfare" and "guerilla tactics" against the Turks have provided a blueprint for counterinsurgency tactics today, and some have said that Lawrence, and not Henry Kissinger, was the first to employ elements of "shuffle diplomacy," wherein which he would use speed as a tactic to go back and forth between different sides to ultimately reach a resolution, whether he was negotiating among various Bedouin tribes or between Faisal and his British superiors.

Though some have blamed Lawrence for being unable to achieve a truly independent Arab state, it must be acknowledged that achievement of such a lofty goal, and one that was met with severe opposition from the most powerful governments of the world at that, was not within one man's power. However, though Faisal was run out of Syria, Lawrence was able to assist in presenting him as a good candidate to rule the British Mandate of Iraq, and Faisal was subsequently King of Iraq from 1921 to 1933. Similarly, Lawrence worked to get Abdullah, the second eldest son of Sharif Hussein, kingship of the new state of Jordan. From 1921-1946, King Abdullah I ruled as Emir of the British Mandate of Jordan, and from 1946 until his assassination in 1951, he ruled as King of an independent Jordan. Though Iraq has since disintegrated and the Hashemite monarchy fell in 1958, the Hashemites continue to rule Jordan today, and the country is comparatively politically stable given the vast instability across the region.

Many lessons can be taken from T.E. Lawrence's legacy and applied to the politics and security of the world today. In a time when the world was still very much divided and imperialist and colonialist thoughts reigned supreme among the minds of many military and government men, Lawrence made a conscious effort to understand the people, culture, and politics of the land he was immersed in. He put himself into the shoes of Faisal, of Sharif Hussein, and of the Bedouin chieftains, and truly sought to see what the world looked like to them. The vastness and depths of the knowledge Lawrence possessed of Arabia were unmatched in comparison to the average American soldier or field commander who walked through the streets of Baghdad during the Iraq War, or the military interpreter who interacted with the network of tribal clans in the mountains of Afghanistan.

At the same time, Lawrence's failures provide key lessons for the world today. One man – however brilliant, knowledgeable, and determined – cannot change an entire world order. It is often overlooked that Lawrence had many supporters who aided his work; frequently, it is assumed that Lawrence was the only influential British officer on the ground, but in truth, he was only one of hundreds of foreign men who played a key role in the Arab Revolt. Additionally, the cooperation of the local people was also an essential component of Lawrence's work. He laid the foundation for a new type of intelligence gathering that prioritized the mapping of tribal networks, as well as direct face-to-face communication instead of communication through interpreters or mediators. Lawrence's extensive utilization of human intelligence, and of the intricate interrelations between various parties, has since been a cornerstone of the counterterrorism efforts of many countries today.

The very fact that new books, documentaries, and articles are still released about T.E. Lawrence and his legacy is indicative of the significant impact he made on the world. Today, with the Middle East and the Arab world experiencing continued instability from the Arab Spring, the Syrian Civil War, and the emergence of the Islamic State in Iraq and the Levant, it is no wonder that many are turning to the legacy of Lawrence for guidance.

1919 portrait of Lawrence by Augustus John

Bibliography

"About Us." *Palestine Exploration Fund.* Accessed November 1, 2014. http://www.pef.org.uk/about/.

Anderson, Scott. *Lawrence in Arabia: War, Deceit, Imperial Folly and the Making of the Modern Middle East.* New York: Anchor Books, 2014.

Browne, O'Brien. "T.E. Lawrence: The Enigmatic Lawrence of Arabia." *Military History.* October 2003. http://www.historynet.com/te-lawrence-the-enigmatic-lawrence-of-arabia.htm.

Carstens, Patrick Richard. *The Encyclopædia of Egypt during the Reign of the Mehemet Ali*

Dynasty 1798-1952: The People, Places and Events that Shaped Nineteenth Century Egypt and its Sphere of Influence. Victoria, BC: Friesen Press, 2104.

Dettmer, Jamie. "Turkish President Declares Lawrence of Arabia a Bigger Enemy than ISIS." *The Daily Beast*. October 13, 2014. http://www.thedailybeast.com/articles/2014/10/13/turkish-president-declares-lawrence-of-arabia-a-bigger-enemy-than-isis.html.

Fromkin, David. *A Peace to End All Peace: The Fall of the Ottoman Empire and the Creation of the Modern Middle East*. New York: Henry Holt and Company, 1989.

"Jordan-Syria Boundary." *International Boundary Study* no. 94. Office of the Geographer, Bureau of Intelligence and Research, 1969.

"King Hussein." *PBS*. Accessed November 5, 2014. http://www.pbs.org/lawrenceofarabia/players/hussein.html.

Korda, Michael. *Hero: The Life and Legacy of Lawrence of Arabia*. New York: Harper Collins, 2010.

Lawrence, T.E. *Seven Pillars of Wisdom: A Triumph*. New York: Knopf Doubleday Publishing Group, 2013.

Liukkonen, Petri. "Who's Who – T.E. Lawrence." *FirstWorldWar.com*. Accessed November 1, 2014. http://www.firstworldwar.com/bio/lawrencete.htm.

"Lowell Thomas." *PBS*. Accessed November 8, 2014. http://www.pbs.org/lawrenceofarabia/players/thomas.html.

"Lowell Thomas, A World Traveler and Broadcaster for 45 Years, Dead." *The New York Times*. August 30, 1981. http://www.nytimes.com/1981/08/30/obituaries/lowell-thomas-a-world-traveler-and-broadcaster-for-45-years-dead.html?pagewanted=3&pagewanted=all.

Mack, John E. *A Prince of Our Disorder: The Life of T.E. Lawrence*. Boston: Harvard University Press, 1998.

Murphy, David. *The Arab Revolt 1916-18: Lawrence Sets Arabia Ablaze*. Oxford: Osprey Publishing, 2008.

Nutting, Anthony. *Lawrence of Arabia: The Man and the Motive*. New York: Signet, 1961.

Orlans, Harold. *T.E. Lawrence: Biography of a Broken Hero*. London: McFarland, 2002.

"Outline Chronology: 1916." *T.E. Lawrence Studies*. Accessed November 5, 2014. http://www.telstudies.org/biography/chron_1916.shtml.

"PEF Annual III: The Wilderness of Zin (revised 3rd edition)." *The Palestine Exploration*

Fund. Accessed November 2, 2014. http://www.pef.org.uk/annuals/the-re-publication-of-the-wilderness-of-zin-pef-annual-iii-by-cl-woolley-and-te-lawrence.

Russell, Malcolm. *The Middle East and South Asia 2014.* Lanham, MD: Rowman & Littlefield, 2014.

Schneider, James. *Guerilla Leader: T.E. Lawrence and the Arab Revolt.* London: Random House, 2011.

Shaw, Stanford J. and Ezel Kural Shaw. *History of the Ottoman Empire and Modern Turkey.* Cambridge: Cambridge University Press, 1977.

Speake, Jennifer. *Literature of Travel and Exploration: An Encyclopedia.* London: Routledge, 2003.

"Strategist of the Desert Dies in Military Hospital: Lord Allenby's Tribute – 'Valued Comrade.'" *The Guardian.* May 19, 1935. http://www.theguardian.com/theguardian/1935/may/19/fromthearchive.

"T.E. Lawrence," *Clio Visualizing History,* http://www.cliohistory.org/thomas-lawrence/lawrence/.

"TE Lawrence (1888-1935)." *BBC.* Accessed November 5, 2014. http://www.bbc.co.uk/history/historic_figures/lawrence_te.shtml.

"The Ottoman Empire: Page 8 – The Arab Revolt, 1916-18)." *NZ History.* Accessed November 5, 2014. http://www.nzhistory.net.nz/war/ottoman-empire/arab-revolt.

"The Sykes-Picot Agreement of 1916." *History Learning Site.* Accessed November 5, 2014. http://www.historylearningsite.co.uk/sykes_picot_agreement.htm.

"The Taking of Akaba." *Clio Visualizing History.* Accessed November 5, 2014. http://www.cliohistory.org/thomas-lawrence/akaba/.

"The Taking of Syria." *Clio Visualizing History.* Accessed November 5, 2014. http://www.cliohistory.org/thomas-lawrence/lawrence/syria/.

Tucker, Spencer C. *The Encyclopedia of World War I.* Santa Barbara: ABC-CLIO, 2005.

Printed in Great Britain
by Amazon